LETTERS FROM
EMILY

A CHRISTIAN WOMAN'S JOURNEY
FROM ABUSE TO FREEDOM
WITH HOPE—JOY—BLESSING

EMILY JUST

WESTBOW
PRESS®
A DIVISION OF THOMAS NELSON
& ZONDERVAN

Scripture quotations marked NRSV are taken from the New Revised Standard Version of the Bible, Copyright 1989, by the Division of Christian Education of the National Council of the Churches of Christ in the United States of America. Used by permission. All rights reserved. Scripture quotations marked TLB are taken from The Living Bible copyright 1971. Used by permission of Tyndale House Publishers, Inc., Carol Stream, Illinois 60188. All rights reserved.

WestBow Press books may be ordered through booksellers or by contacting:

WestBow Press
A Division of Thomas Nelson & Zondervan
1663 Liberty Drive
Bloomington, IN 47403
www.westbowpress.com
1 (866) 928-1240

ISBN: 978-1-5127-8543-2 (sc)
ISBN: 978-1-5127-8567-8 (hc)
ISBN: 978-1-5127-8544-9 (e)

Library of Congress Control Number: 2017906894

Print information available on the last page.

WestBow Press rev. date: 05/10/2017

PREFACE

These letters from Emily are written from a Christian woman's experience and the insights she gained in the journey of a long marriage that became abusive. Divorce followed. She shares the spiritual journey. Each letter is addressed to Angela, an unknown woman who is struggling with abuse. To maintain anonymity, no names or specific locations are used.

It is a semi-chronological look at the journey. Faith, family, and friends were her companions. Hope energized her. Grace made the journey possible. Years of journaling helped map the journey. She has been blessed and is so grateful. These letters are Emily's way of reaching out to others with love and encouragement.

It's good to be safe and free. It's good to be joyful and smile!

CONTENTS

1

Why?

It was a long journey from abuse to freedom. Prayer was a wonderful gift along the way, which was often lonely and scary. There were many questions: Why? Why us? Why me? What now? How long? What next?

At first I set some boundaries, which were too weak and too few. Then I tried denying that there was a problem. Some understanding of the paradox of life and the need for balance helped me recognize reality. To be centered in Christ was the clear path. Love, grace, and forgiveness protected me.

Why, Lord?
Out of Bounds
The Elephant's Not Elegant
Life in "Baladox"—The Teeter-Totter
In the Midst of Our Mess—Grace
Scars Are

Why, Lord?

Dear Angela,

Thank you for letting me share my thoughts with you. I am so sorry you find yourself in an abusive marriage. You don't deserve to be abused! Abuse is evil. It is never okay. It is not God's plan.

The reality of abuse came to me as a big surprise. I thought it was something that happened to others. Likewise, divorce was not anticipated. Naïveté and some overconfidence in my ability to succeed at almost anything distorted reality. I spent decades in pain struggling with abuse. I tried to be better, I prayed, I hoped, and I yearned for peace and joy.

It seemed so never-ending and lonely. I appreciate the struggle you are experiencing. What has been constant throughout my journey is faith. God has always loved me and my abuser too. God loves the sinner. God hates the sin. We are all loved. We are sometimes tested. We are never tested beyond what we can bear. God provides strength and direction in the toughest of places. The abuse is over. I am blessed and joyful.

I will write to you often. And in the letters that follow, I will share with you and pray it will encourage you. I asked many questions along the way. Some questions were easy to answer; some were very intense with no quick answer. Others have been left with God in prayer. God's time is the best time for answers. Now, there are many vignettes of blessing and joy in my life. This is how my story began.

Loving, Christian parents provided my home growing up. I grew up an only child, often lonely but surrounded by Christian friends and family. I knew nothing of abusive relationships in our family, community, or church family. As a teenager, I was playing music for worship services and teaching individual lessons. I became a schoolteacher, did graduate study, taught at a college, and worked in churches and later for the government in social welfare.

I didn't date in high school, and college dating was limited. My great desire was to marry and be a mommy. In my twenties, I married. It didn't seem like an ideal relationship. However, I had rejected other relationships and thought it was time to marry and become the wife and mommy I so wanted to be. That marriage of a dozen years had some wonderful times, and I became a mommy to two children. I am so grateful. It was a complicated relationship, and it ended in divorce. Spiritually, it was most devastating. I was such a sinner to have failed. But my Savior was there and rescued me.

There were years of single parenting, employment struggles, and limited socialization. I tried to make a careful postmortem of the first marriage and move thoughtfully into a return to dating. Many years later, there was a second marriage. Domestic abuse evolved. There were so many questions: *Why, Lord? Why us? Why me? What now? How long? What next?* Prayers for forgiveness and guidance accompanied the journey.

I will write again soon with more of the story of good times, joyous times, and the transition into the darkness of abuse and out into safety and blessing. Each of my letters will focus on specific issues and questions. Abuse is not a unique experience. We need others. It's not good to travel alone.

Take care. Trust your Lord to guide you.

Emily

OUT OF BOUNDS

Dear Angela,

When you married, you were probably quite happy. Now, are you asking, "What happened?" My second marriage was a welcome event. After years alone, I learned to love and be loved, to care, to share, and to grow together. When we first met, we asked each other a lot of questions, much like a job interview. We had both been married and divorced and had children. His were older. My son was still in high school. We talked for hours about anything and everything. It felt good. It was so special to share conversation, to go places and do things together, and to worship together. It was good to be loved, appreciated, and respected. It was good to love, appreciate, and respect him.

We went to premarital counseling. My pastor was a bit concerned that both of us were perhaps a little too confident in the success of the marriage. He made some suggestions. He told us the best secret in marriage was no secret. We agreed. He also suggested we lighten up. We were both serious. I thought we were serious because we were responsible and honest. Perhaps it came from insecurity. To lighten up could mean vulnerability. We tried to relax and not be quite so serious.

Early on, we were together excessively. We shopped together for groceries and whatever household needs we had. He even went with me to shop for clothing. I was expected to account for every penny spent. I resented this. I had an excellent full-time job and two part-time jobs. I was a good money manager, a careful shopper, and certainly trustworthy. I did set a boundary on this, and it worked. However, it was one of the few boundaries I set in our relationship.

He had few friends. When he took early retirement, the friendships fell apart, and eventually he had none. My friends were close, and we did a lot together. He resented my friends and tried to isolate me. I refused to give up my friends. We continued to get together frequently and still do. I did limit how often they came to our house. Note: I didn't say home. He owned the property before we married, and it never felt like home because of his restrictions. That boundary with friends was mostly good.

Not too far into our marriage, he objected to my children. My son was forced to move out with inadequate education and employment. My daughter was barely tolerated when she came to visit. Eventually, he would tell me I was not a good mother, not a real mother. This was because my children were adopted. He said his family was better than my family—no comparison.

As he became increasingly unhappy, he would not allow my daughter's family to come to the house. That was nonnegotiable. I was not to spend a nickel on them. Later, my son couldn't come either; my husband was just being "fair." When I was upset about not being able to be with my grandchildren, he told me there were programs where I could adopt a grandchild instead. This rift went on for years. I didn't set a boundary soon enough.

I tried to deny the abuse. I wondered if I was too sensitive. Maybe I could try harder. I tried to fix the relationship with my family. I tried to see my family elsewhere. I needed to protect them, especially the grandchildren, from his abuse. Not only had I not set a boundary, there was an elephant in the room ready to charge. I prayed and struggled with guilt, weakness, pain, and sadness. Gradually my faith, family, and friends led me to own it for what it was. Forgiveness and grace helped me move on and find help, strength, and courage. More in my next letter.

Be aware,

Emily

THE ELEPHANT'S NOT ELEGANT

Dear Angela,

My last letter was about denying abuse and not setting good boundaries. I was so ashamed and in so much pain. Still, I didn't want everyone to know the reality of the elephant. If you can't see the elephant, maybe it doesn't exist.

Maybe the elephant will go away.
Maybe I can hide the elephant.
Elephants eat a lot.
Elephants never forget.
Elephants need space. This elephant is out of place.
What do you do with an elephant?

When I first tried to hide the elephant, I was working a full-time day job. After work, I was self-employed in music with children. I loved it. It was refreshing, energizing, and fun, and it took me away from the pain.

I couldn't hide the elephant forever. The abuse escalated. The elephant hurt me. The abuse changed from a mostly private behavior at home to public places as well. It became more intense. It hurt. It frightened me. It broke my heart.

The presence of the elephant was anything but elegant. I needed to get rid of the elephant or leave. I was afraid of the elephant.

In my next letters, I will share some of the first attempts to do this.

Angela, please don't try to hide the elephant. There are better options.

Wishing you well,

Emily

LIFE IN "BALADOX"—
THE TEETER-TOTTER

Dear Angela,

Abusers leave us feeling so rotten. Put-downs, blame games, and all sorts of abusive acts put us off balance. Coping with an abuser is a daunting task. It's not a do-it-all-by-yourself project. Still, if you don't act, it won't end. It's a paradox.

The Christian life is filled with paradox. Perhaps it's saint and sinner; holding close or letting go; or down and out and up, up, and away. The seeming opposites in life that define each other are better understood when we find balance. That is life in "baladox."

Balance is essential and beautiful. I think of balance as being like playing on a teeter-totter. You need someone else to play with you, unless you are content to always be on the bottom, be bumped off, or you are willing to stand in the middle and maintain equal weight and motion. That's not fun.

The point of balance is the fulcrum. Christ is the fulcrum point. We need to recognize our centeredness. As we teeter-totter through life, whatever action we take alone or with others is futile without balance.

The teeter-totter is a paradox. Up and down, down and up, each defines the other, and they never have the same position. Like the "Grand Old Duke of York," "Oh, when you're up, you're up, and when you're down, you're down. And when you're only halfway up, you're neither up nor down." No teeter-totter has all ups or downs. If it did, it could neither teeter nor totter, or perhaps it would always teeter and totter.

Balance is not having all ups or downs. Balance denotes equality, centeredness, and abundance. Centered in Christ, we are all equal, and that is clearly the evidence of God's always abundant love. God's love supply is inexhaustible.

Abuse is off balance. It is not centered. It is not God's plan.

When I complained about the abuse in the marriage, I had to remember that God loves both of us. But God does not love abusive behavior. It is evil.

Angela, be patient. Trust and rely on Christ to be the center, to help you. You are loved. Forgive as you are forgiven. In my next letter, I want to share more.

Be centered in Christ,

IN THE MIDST OF OUR
MESS—GRACE

Dear Angela,

Abuse is a mess. It is out-of-control life clutter. Most of the abuse that I experienced was a control issue. It was behavior to try to overcome fear, anxiety, depression. Manipulation, deceit, control, isolation, name-calling, threats, using, and abusing were all blatantly selfish. Abusive behavior is devoid of empathy.

Abuse left me in a mess. My heart was broken, as I am sure yours is as well. I asked God, "Why?" I asked for strength. When Jesus came to us as a baby, he came in the midst of our mess. Stables are not very hygienic. Neither are our hearts.

Sometimes my barn, my stable, has been a shabby, smelly shelter for my soul. Only when I let the Lord take me and snuggle me in his arms and protect me from all that would destroy me can I be transformed, be safe, be free, and be loving. In the midst of our mess, perhaps especially in our mess, we are loved.

Love is a gift wrapped in many ways. Abusers mock love and forgiveness; that is sick and evil. But God is not mocked. When abuse was so heavy in my life and life was so messy, God didn't leave me. Faith and family and friends rescued me. Grace came. It's always good to embrace grace.

It was hard to ask for help. I was so mired in the ugly mess. How could I escape?

There can be no room for grudge. Grace is a gift. Grudge is a trudge. Make grace the pace. God's time is best.

Grace to you,

Emily

SCARS ARE

Dear Angela,

Does forgiving seem futile? Abusers just keep at it. It seems lopsided, like I should forgive you for making me out to be the worthless one who is the real problem, the big problem. Forgiving another, especially an abuser, can be very difficult, but there is no excuse not to forgive.

Sometimes when we need to forgive, we get trapped into thinking the wrongdoer doesn't deserve forgiveness. Wrong! If there had been no wrongdoing, there would be no need for forgiveness. Right needs no forgiveness. We are sinners flawed and saints forgiven—what a beautiful paradox.

When I was a little girl, I broke my mother's very special mixing bowl. I remember it as a rather ordinary, mottled blue and gray bowl. I don't know how I broke it. Maybe I dropped it or was careless or ... I was so sorry I broke it and hurt her feelings. She was disappointed the bowl was broken, but she forgave me freely. Soon after, my grandmother took me shopping for Mom's birthday, and we found a set of bowls. Mom treasured the new bowls. What a beautiful memory.

"Forgive us our trespasses as we forgive those who trespass against us." How many times have I been forgiven? How many times have I forgiven? It defies recordkeeping. It is grace, it is love, and it is generosity—an un-quantified gift to give and to receive.

More and more, I realize that forgetting about what is broken—relationships, things, a person's heart—is not the essence of forgiveness. Forgiveness knows what to forget and what to remember. Forgiveness makes way for healing a broken anything. Sometimes the injury or the scar shouldn't be forgotten, not as an excuse to hold a grudge but to provide a catalyst for more caring and loving behavior. What needs to be forgotten is hatred.

Forgiveness remembers Easter and the resurrection, the joy of salvation. When Christ said to forgive them because they didn't know what they were doing, it wasn't to make an excuse for them. It was hope. They were promised paradise. Forgiveness is the power to move on, trusting in God's goodness.

Forgiveness given or received *forgets* hatred. Forgiveness given or received *remembers* faith, hope, and love.

Angela, do not deny the pain, injury, and hurt you are feeling. Work on healing and recovery and renewal. Scars are! Christ did not deny the scars, the hurt, and the pain. Christ forgave. Ask Christ to hold your hand and lead you. Stop dragging your feet. Ask the Holy Spirit to manage your mouth. Witness to God's love. Be thankful for strength and healing. Live with love, patience, joy, and generosity. Remember hope and promise. Our Lord and Savior cares.

Wishing you strength and courage,

Emily

2

Now What?

Honesty. Early in the marriage, I needed to be honest with myself. The marriage was deteriorating. How could I live with this? Could it be fixed? At first, I was quietly bullied about by many things. Then there were attacks on my soul. It imprisoned me in yet another way.

Clearly, help was needed. I avoided conflict, kept my distance, and tried not to irritate or agitate. I shared a little of the pain with a pastor and close friends. I prayed and tried to listen. I asked my husband how we could make it better. His basic nonresponse was a roadblock.

Tell It Like It Is
The Big Bully Battle
Imprisonment of the Heart—Breaking Free
The Reluctant Tattletale
Time-Out
Can We Make It Better? What Do You Really Want?

TELL IT LIKE IT IS

Dear Angela,

Perhaps my last letter to you seemed harsh. I hope not. It took me a long time to understand forgiveness like that. Forgiving and being forgiven provided a solid foundation for change. We come to God as sinners flawed and then are blessed as saints forgiven.

My abuser often tried to silence me. Journaling helped me cope with the domestic abuse. I documented facts, thoughts, feelings, and questions. I vented, I prayed, I made plans, and I often grieved. In short, the journals were for reflecting, evaluating, exploring, and pursuing.

There were good times noted in the extended journals. There was a separate daily journal: *Faith, Family & Friends—Grace & Gratitude*. Here I recorded at least three good things for each day. These were often single-word entries like, "chocolate, sunrise, laughter." I still do this, and the perspective is very helpful. It is a journey of the heart. Wisdom often comes from heart thought.

Writing clarified the complicated reality of the marriage. It was a way to express my needs, my fears, my joys, my sorrow, and my hope. It fostered reality: tell it like it is.

I wanted to understand why there were the abuse issues. I wanted to know what to do. I wanted help.

In my next letters, I will share some of the journaling thoughts.

Take care,

Emily

THE BIG BULLY BATTLE

Dear Angela,

My abuser often behaved like a bully. Does the bully stand for right or wrong? Does the bully think, *Fight, be strong?*

When my daughter was very young, a neighbor boy would stand in the middle of the sidewalk and not let her pass. No matter how often she tried, it was still a no-passing zone. One day, I told her not to try to pass but let him stand there until he got tired of it. It didn't take long. Sometimes patience works, and other times not. Then it's time to find another way.

Bully behavior is all about the use and abuse of power and/or the lack of power.

Only the abuser can stop the bad behavior. I tried to enable and encourage change. It seemed like a plan. I tried to be understanding, helpful, flexible, responsible, and grateful. I tried to be better. Bottom line: I wanted the abuse to stop. I needed to find another way.

Abuse is pervasive, hurtful behavior in word and action or neglect. When I first thought he was abusing me, I made excuses for both of us. If I could excuse or call it something else, maybe it wasn't abuse or maybe it would go away. Recognizing abuse went like this:

1. Denial.
2. Maybe he doesn't know any better.
3. Maybe he doesn't know it hurts me.
4. Maybe he thinks and/or I am too sensitive.
5. Maybe he knows but thinks it's not that important.
6. Maybe I can be better. Maybe I expect too much.
7. Maybe I can just ignore the behavior.
8. Maybe he can't help it.
9. He knows what he is doing, and hurting me is okay, even desirable.
10. No change in sight, and it's not safe.

Abuse is not okay. I had to find another way.

Be careful,

IMPRISONMENT OF THE
HEART—BREAKING FREE

Dear Angela,

Abuse is always spiritual abuse of personhood. I think abusers choose to attack the soul above all else. If our will can't be destroyed by controlling our behavior, then isolating the heart and soul is another abuser tactic.

For many years, we attended church together. At first, he said he felt better after church. Gradually, he ragged on worship, pastors, the church people, me, my faith, love, and forgiveness. The after-church commentary was just plain ugly. I dreaded this and wondered why he went to church when it so annoyed him. Later, he didn't.

I prayed for our well-being, for patience, for strength, for courage, and for forgiveness. I thanked God for love, for forgiveness and grace.

He based his complaints on human naïveté, the lack of logic, and the historical inaccuracy of the Bible. He questioned a good God letting bad things happen. He didn't like my answers to his questions. My response was that faith had mystery—that if I totally understood

God there would be no need for God. God is real. God is omnipotent, all loving, forgiving, and eternal. I believe God is the creator, and the creator is greater than the creation. He had agnostic thoughts. I shared my thoughts about agnostics and atheists. If a person believes there is no God, then that person has assumed ultimate power with wisdom to make that assumption. Is the atheist trying to be a self-appointed God? That is arrogance, and self-appointment is blasphemy.

In our very inmost heart, there is a yearning to be free. For the Christian, the soul can never be silenced. Imprisonment is humbling. Prayer is the conduit to freedom. That was the way of breaking free.

Be free,

Emily

THE RELUCTANT TATTLETALE

Dear Angela,

Well, it never seems right to be a tattletale. When I first admitted to myself that ours was a deteriorating marriage, I knew help was needed. It wasn't that I expected too much. It wasn't because I was too sensitive. How could I get help? Who could help?

I felt betrayed, demoted, unworthy, disappointed, scared, and somewhat helpless. Talking to a pastor seemed a lot like being a tattletale. I think we both tried to hide. My husband did not hold the church and pastors in high regard. He eventually worked with a therapist but didn't follow through with additional referrals. I prayed. I knew I couldn't keep it a total secret. One of the first things I did was send an anonymous postcard to our church requesting prayers for the abused and their abusers.

My closest friends were told about the abuse. They were kind and supportive. They respected privacy. I was supported by prayers.

Eventually I spoke with one of our pastors. I felt like a tattletale because he wasn't just my pastor; he was his pastor too. It didn't seem quite right. I asked for prayers, and the pastor was kind and prayed.

Few knew of the abuse. I found a therapist who was also a Christian and musician and who helped me immensely. Gradually, more people knew, including my family. It was not a surprise to them. They were helpful.

There were more visits with pastors, who were great helpers.

In retrospect, maybe I wasn't a tattletale. I needed a rescue team.

Angela, going it alone is too heavy.

Others care,

Emily

Time-Out

Dear Angela,

Are you tired of abuse? Take some time out. Take care of you.

I hate conflict. I don't like to fight. He often ranted. His verbal stuff was full of excuses, pettiness, and blaming. He said I always wanted to fight, I needed to learn how to get along with people, I paused when I talked, I talked too slowly, I took too long to get to the point. If I questioned the abuse, he would blame me for whatever, call me cruel and ugly names, tell me I talked too much, prattled and chattered, and the list went on.

He would always defend his behavior. He would tell me I was hard to be around and suggest I leave for a while. One fall when he had made me quite unwelcome at home, he softened before Thanksgiving and gave me permission to stay at home if I had no place else to go. When I reminded him that he had once said I was a fine person, he responded with that was before he knew me. Long after that Thanksgiving, I wondered if leaving then would have been better.

Self-defense was futile. Was it wimpy to hide from the sight and sounds of abusive behavior? I knew I deserved better treatment. I took time out to regroup.

There were coping skills that were helpful. I read a lot. I did journaling. I wrote teaching materials for my students. I traveled online to other lands and places. Occasionally I took a nap.

It was good to go out with friends, work part-time, volunteer, and garden. Music was wonderful: I listened, I played, I taught, and I composed. I was allowed limited time with my family. I worshipped regularly.

Daily devotions started my day. Morning was my time. He wasn't up early. It was so peaceful and beautiful. Occasionally I caught the sunrise. It was attitude-adjustment time and a new day! I asked Christ to take my hand and lead me, and for the Holy Spirit to manage my mouth. At the end of each day, I noted three good things in my *Faith, Family & Friends—Grace & Gratitude* journal.

I tried not to talk very much. If I couldn't talk to him about anything and everything that mattered to me, at least some of the time, it was easier to be quiet. Too much went unacknowledged, discounted, or he would interrupt me midsentence, even midword. Maybe he didn't hear, maybe didn't care, and maybe he just chose to ignore me. I didn't like being told, "Shut up your mouth." He said I didn't listen to him, and sometimes I did just let him go on with his negative monologues. Why bother? Most responses were ignored or negated.

One day, he asked sarcastic questions about my driving. My driving was fine. I chose not to answer.

Then he demanded, "Answer me!" I did not. I would not be obedient to his command.

The many angry words were painful. I felt devalued. It devastated me and pushed me away. I wanted happiness, and that was how I tried to be. More and more, I knew a longer time-out was needed. It would be game over.

Angela, you deserve to be treated well!

Take care,

Emily

Can We Make It Better?
What Do You Really Want?

Dear Angela,

Do you question yourself about abuse? Victims of abuse seem to have a lot in common. We do have different ways of coping. It's good to ask why, to listen well, and to see clearly the dynamics of the situation. You deserve better. Trying to engage the abuser in a plan doesn't work very often, but it will answer some of your questions about the abuser's commitment to change. When the abuser is disengaged, it's time for the abused to engage. An abusive relationship is never stagnant.

Good questions need good answers. Conversation, as you know from my last letter, wasn't working well. Several years ago, I asked these tough questions about our marriage. When I asked these questions, they weren't answered well. I wanted the abuse to end and a positive plan to evolve. I asked what we could do to make it better. I asked what he wanted. There wasn't much response.

Good answers remained elusive. I still think they were good questions, and what follows is what surrounded the questions. The process helped me better understand the dynamics of our marriage. I had to accept that minimal response was not what I wanted, but it was an answer to both questions.

He knew frequent soul-searching always led me to focus on faith, family, and friends. I wanted a life of living, loving, caring, and sharing. God's love and grace allowed me to be forgiven, to be set free and empowered to move on. Every day, I recorded at least three good things or thoughts in my journal. It helped to be positive and grateful for blessings. Prayer was inspiration, guidance, and comfort.

I reminded him that when we married, I expected to love and be loved, to work through differences in a respectful, helpful way. I expected to encourage and be encouraged, to comfort and be comforted, to be honest and caring, and to be affectionate and kind. It didn't go that way very long.

My husband knew I didn't like isolation. He liked to be in control. I so wanted to share my joys and sorrows with him, but that was discouraged. I tried to be a good listener. It was best not to question or disagree about anything. There were off-limits topics, including talk about my family. When I was criticized for talking too much, I tried to talk less, listen more, and adjust. When I asked for feedback on my reduced talking, he complained about weeks of silence. I tried to find things

I enjoyed and found relaxing. He criticized these choices as well.

There was a lot of disrespect and rudeness in word and deed. He was often in my face or in my personal space. Name-calling and put-downs were common. The angry, screaming abuse often left me devastated and in tears. After the outbursts, sleep was difficult. There were far too many outbursts. When I asked him how he felt after the outbursts, he said he felt better. I didn't. An apology was rare. Defending his own abusive behavior became more frequent.

Still, I tried to exercise responsible behavior. I freely admitted I made mistakes and needed forgiveness. I tried to understand, to rationalize, and even to make excuses for his behavior. I didn't want to believe he could be so blatantly abusive. Sometimes I just tried to take it and say nothing. That was one way of avoiding immediate conflict. It was like using a vacuum cleaner for quick cleanup. It works. But keep doing it, and sooner or later you end up with a dirty old bag full of ugly stuff.

I told him loving was not just when you got your own way or when it was easy. Sometimes it was just plain hard work. Compassion accompanied by compromise was not part of the picture. In so many ways, he betrayed and devalued me as a person and his wife. Affection was all but gone. He blamed me for being an inadequate wife. It seemed to me that his concept of loving and intimacy was limited to a sexual intimacy. I wondered if there had ever been a time when he had truly loved me as a whole person. I felt so unloved and so unwanted I went to the other bedroom. I felt sad, cheap, and angry with myself for trusting him with my heart.

The blame game was rampant. It wasn't all my fault, other people's fault, or his either. I had asked if we could make it better. I had asked what he really wanted. He said he didn't understand. I tried to understand what he didn't or didn't want to understand. I felt good about making the effort. It felt honest, not like I was harboring a secret about my feelings. I had hoped we could communicate. I wanted us to love and care for each other in the best way possible.

It was a disappointing time. It never got better.

Angela, as you journey, take time to be kind to yourself, especially as you experience the difficult and disappointing times.

Be strong,

Emily

3

Help!

Avoiding conflict. Acquiescence was the weak way. It didn't work. When rejection and betrayal are rampant, it clearly doesn't work to take flexibility and submission to extremes. My wants and needs got so mixed up that too many weeds emerged. This was part of the crop failure.

Abuse became pervasive. Nonetheless, I chose to acquiesce. The abuse escalated. Sadness invaded the depths of my being. I prayed for strength and patience. I begged the Lord for help. I prayed, asking the Lord to help me understand what to do.

Acquiescence—Stuck in the Mess
Death of Passion
Trustworthy
Wants and Needs—I Nurtured Weeds
So Sorry, No Sorry, No Honeymoon
Over the Top
Jesus Wept—Me Too
Do You Hear Me, Lord? Help Me
Understand What You're Saying.

Acquiescence—Stuck
in the Mess

Dear Angela,

When I wrote the last letter, I told you it hadn't gotten better. That was true. For a time after that, I craved affection and an "I love you." That changed too. I was stuck in a mess and too willing to acquiesce. I no longer believed that he loved me. The craving went away.

Gradually, I became increasingly good at acquiescence. I could often sense the tension rising and would try to stay away, accept it for what it was, and hope it would dissipate. It rarely did. One afternoon after an outburst of much of the same old stuff and some new stuff, more of the blame game and put-downs, I went out to sit on the deck and just be still. He came to the door, opened it, and started in again. I didn't want to be trapped with no stairway for escape, so I came in, and he continued. Reasoning with an abuser is futile. I tried to say I was sorry for sometimes being too edgy. There was just more angry criticism of me. He left for a walk. I played the piano.

I wasn't very assertive. Self-care is not the same

as being defensive. It is good to listen for feedback and suggestion but always remember who you are. I no longer allow others to dismiss or devalue my thoughts, feelings, and choices. I can trust myself to act wisely and correct my actions as needed. It is not a sense of exaggerated entitlement or arrogance that motivates me.

There was a time when I worked in an otherwise all-male department. The chairman told me I was their "token woman." My response was silence. I wonder what his response would have been if I had said, "You're partly right. I am a woman, but I'm not your token anything." In terms of job security, silence was probably the right choice. But it's okay to believe I am a good person. Self-respect and self-confidence require this positive perspective. It's okay to be bully-resistant. It's okay to talk back. It just takes practice and patience to learn effective ways to be assertive.

To acquiesce may not be the same as to submit. About the same time, my husband had told me the Bible says wives are to be in submission to their husbands. I reminded him that Paul didn't stop with instructions for wives. If he had, that would certainly be a basis for control and even abuse of wives. But husbands are to love their wives as Christ loves the church and as a man loves his own body.

Angela, if you're stuck in a mess, it doesn't work to acquiesce. I wanted to submit to loving kindness and care, to not simply be weak and try to take what was dished out. Too often, I submitted to use and abuse. My assertiveness skills were minimal. My acquiescence was part of the mess.

Be brave,

Emily

DEATH OF PASSION

Dear Angela,

You and I both know that abuse inflicts serious injury. You deserve to find help and healing. I do wish you well. I hope you can survive and thrive.

Early in our relationship and marriage, there was deep passion, love, and affection. Gradually, abuse destroyed trust. I felt rejected, lonely, and isolated. It was no longer a healthy home. I repeatedly suggested that we seek counsel together and/or individually. He was unwilling. He didn't want me to go to a therapist either. After I did, he said it didn't help because it hadn't solved our problem.

His anger scared me. One time, to get away from an angry outburst, I went to another room. He followed me and was so enraged and in my face that his spittle hit my face. There were angry comments about my belief in love and forgiveness. Love and forgiveness are essential. It is wrong to be mean-spirited and hateful. When I asked why he deliberately treated me and spoke to me in such abusive ways, his answer was essentially that I deserved it. Abusive behavior is never acceptable. You never deserve to be abused! Never!

He would tell me I didn't get it. He suggested/threatened divorce several times. That wasn't what I wanted. I wanted to live peacefully and productively. I wanted to talk freely, to be affirmed for the good, and to be forgiven for the bad. There had been a time when we talked about nearly everything; we were affectionate and enjoyed each other's company. He withheld affection. One time, I calmly asked him if he thought he would ever feel affection for me again. He asked why I asked. I said because I wanted to know. He did not answer me.

I told him I would not ask for affection again because if he didn't feel it, I didn't want it.

I tried to be patient and understand. The blame game, pity party, and guilt trips continued. I was embarrassed and saddened. I felt like a failure. The angry outbursts became more and more stressful, and physical ills followed, although I tried to be calm. My blood pressure went up significantly. I had muscle spasms in my back, hips, legs, and gut. I was hospitalized after syncope. Sometimes I'd vomit and couldn't sleep.

It wasn't until I honestly recognized and accepted the relationship for what it wasn't that I could move on. He was doing nothing, which let me believe or feel he loved me. It was the death of passion. I deserved better.

Angela, be kind to yourself. Know that you deserve better.

Be aware,

TRUSTWORTHY

Dear Angela,

What next? Is there no end to the abusive behavior? Abusers attack in so many ways. I still don't understand the attack on trust.

I trusted my husband with my heart. Bummer. He broke my heart.

I trusted my husband to be honest and forthright. He managed our finances and managed them well. Even so, when he decided to make changes in my individual accounts without discussing it with me, I was disgusted. The financial decisions were fine. Finding out after the fact seemed sneaky and very disrespectful.

I trusted my husband to be truthful. He would make statements about things that just were not true. It was common with excuse making and sometimes with crazy making. When I objected, there was little response.

I trusted my husband to value me.

Trustworthy people don't habitually hurt others.

Be alert,

Wants and Needs—I
Nurtured Weeds

Dear Angela,

In the midst of abuse, I got lost. I ended up in a big patch of weeds. There were many things I wanted in marriage. There were many things I needed. I wanted my needs met. Wants and needs are not the same thing. Wants can go on a wish list like a letter to Santa Claus. A wish list has options. Some things on my wish list / want list were good wants. Needs aren't options. My needs were too often pushed aside. I denied my needs in the marriage because I didn't want to be demanding. I wanted to love, to give, and to share. I trusted I would be loved and treated well.

I was good at acquiescence but not good at risk-taking. Part of me succumbed to the doormat syndrome. Rejection was frightening. I didn't want to be selfish and insist on my own way. I wanted to always do my fair share and expected he would do the same.

We are to first love God and then our neighbor as ourselves. If you don't love yourself, the neighbor gets a raw deal. Too often, I didn't take care of me. I mixed up my wants and my needs. I nurtured weeds. Weeds were part of the crop failure.

Take care of your needs,

Emily

So Sorry, No Sorry, No Honeymoon

Dear Angela,

Have you ever wondered about "Sorry"? In abusive relationships, that word is not frequent. When you do hear it, careful scrutiny is revealing. Five kinds of sorry:

1. Etiquette faux pas
2. Perfunctory for minor misdeed
3. Sincere for unintended misdeed even of a more serious nature, regret included
4. Empty with no "skin" in the word
5. Deceitful

The deceitful sorry is the abusive one. Once after my husband had spoken to me unkindly and I objected, he said he was sorry. I thought about it. It seemed a little questionable and flat. I asked what he was sorry about; he told me he was sorry because I didn't like his words, and I didn't like his tone. He wasn't sorry about how he treated me. He was sorry because I didn't like his unkindness. So sorry, no sorry.

Is the sorry to take you to a more peaceful place? I suppose abusers get tired too. Maybe that's why there is literature and talk about the honeymoon time in the abuse cycle. Does your abuser need time to regroup before the next attack? Sorry buys time? I think that once there is a habit of abuse in a relationship, the abuse is 24/7 and 365. Shoes come in pairs. Once the first shoe drops, it's most likely the second one will also drop. It may be quiet for a time, but in reality, more abuse is likely. In between the bouts of aggression, the abuse continues as residual stress and fear even in the quiet time. There is no honeymoon.

Listen to your heart,

Emily

Over the Top

Dear Angela,

I hope you are in a safe place. I hope you are not pretending all is well when it isn't.

Abusive anger and rage were torments from the early days until the final days. There were threats and repeated suggestions of divorce. He would be so angry he was literally foaming at the mouth. One time he was lying on the floor in fetal position. He didn't confine the outbursts of anger and rage to our home. This happened at the mall, at church, before a recital, at a restaurant, and in his therapist's office. He often expressed death wishes and talked of suicide, once even suggesting we both get in the car with the garage door closed. More than once when I asked how I could help him, he gestured and said, "Shoot me." He wished he'd never been born. There were panic attacks.

Physical illness in later years complicated the behavior. The mental health issues with the pervasive negative attitude, fear, anxiety, and depression were difficult to manage for both of us.

From the get-go, I told him that physical abuse was a deal breaker. He told me he had physically abused his first wife. I wanted to believe that since he was so up front about it that he had changed and it wouldn't be a problem.

However, physical abuse is an insidious intruder. Years ago, the woman who was my therapist told me that she considered physical illness, such as elevated blood pressure, to be physical abuse. As I wrote in an earlier letter, there were several physical illnesses that clearly followed the abusive treatment I'd experienced.

Early on, there was a shove of my arm, later a hard pinch. There was spittle in my face. He hit me in bed with a flailing arm; that may have been in part from a medication side effect. He came at me with glaring eyes and frightening body language. I put my hands up in front of my face and told him repeatedly not to touch me until he backed off. He shoved a rolling chair violently across the kitchen. One day he gave me a crushing hug. It was scary, and I pleaded for him to release me. He asked if I thought he was pretty strong. The next day, he said I needed another hug. I told him not if it was like the previous.

Months later, he raised a fist, and again I told him not to touch me. Another time, I had gone to another room and closed the door. He entered anyway. The day before I left him, he blocked the doorway of our office. I got past him and went to work at the dining room table. He then plopped stuff down on top of my bookkeeping. I moved it, and he did it again.

That was the moment of decision. I couldn't stay. I

would leave the next day. He would later suggest that because he hadn't really slugged me, there wasn't abuse.

Lots of stuff had seemed over the top. The day before I left, I knew I had to leave. His behavior was over the top. I was in way over my head.

Stay safe,

Emily

Jesus Wept—Me Too

Dear Angela,

My heart says you've shed a lot of tears. Tears are not shameful. Cry—cry out to God!

Our abusers know all too well how to push the tears button. For them, it's a power and control button. We know the power of "Hear my cry, O Lord." We know the pain of deliberate hurt. We know the abuser's skill to use our tears against us. We know abusers label tears as weakness on our part. Our abusers don't want to own the pain and tears they cause. We know our abuser's inability and/or unwillingness to respond to our pain and tears in a helpful way. We know how much release from stress can come with tears. It's not self-pity. Sadness needs release.

My abuser told me tears were weakness. I don't think so. Sometimes he would hurt me so deeply the tears would come. Then he would criticize my tears as something wrong with my feelings, not his behavior. My abuser seemed to get pleasure from making me cry. It was better to not let him see me cry. Tears were often near the surface, but I cried elsewhere. I didn't want to give him that pleasure. There were lots of tears before we divorced. When the divorce was final, I felt profound sadness. I wept. There is still pain, but God has forgiven me, and I have forgiven my former husband. There are still tears but not so much now. It helps to let go and let God.

Tears are an expression from the depths of our soul. Jesus wept in sadness over the city. That wasn't weakness. It wasn't self-pity. I think it was God's love and care expressed in the humanity of Jesus.

As we move away from abuse, we can anticipate freedom, happiness, safety, music, laughter, and joy. The sun rises on the new day. Tears of joy are good.

Let go, let God,

Emily

Do You Hear Me, Lord?
Help Me Understand
What You're Saying.

Dear Angela,

How do we pray about abuse? In years of journaling, I wrote many prayers. Many of them were please and thank-you prayers. Please: I asked for a lot. Thank you: I received a lot. Yes, I know the Lord hears us. We are also promised that the Holy Spirit intercedes for us when we don't know how to pray or what to pray for. That helped me understand what the Lord was saying.

In my journey through abuse to freedom, I first prayed for help in the marriage. When the marriage deteriorated and I decided to leave, I prayed for forgiveness for leaving. When I understood that the marriage covenant, not the legal document, had really been broken years ago, I prayed for forgiveness for staying so long.

Sometimes I was annoyed and impatient. I felt wasted and worthless. I had to admit this and deal with it before things would get better. I had to back up and ask, who is God? God is. I am not God. God is good.

God is in control. God is the giver. God is love. God is the source of forgiveness and grace.

God's time is best.

Be patient,

Emily

4

Could I? Should I? Would I?

Decision: these three questions helped me understand what I would do. The abuse had to end. What were my choices?

Planning: there were more questions. What did I need? Was I ready to travel in a new direction? Was I strong enough in body, mind, and soul? Who could help me? Most of all, there was prayer, asking the Lord to help me make right choices, to help me understand how to live with the choice, to make a plan. There was hope for an end to the abuse.

No—Yes
Lost—Where Is Home?
How Are You?
How Do I Look?
Do I Need a Jacket?
Thin Ice and Eggshells
Flight Delay
Be Well Nourished! Fruit Is Good!
Ducks in a Row: Could I? Should I? Would I?

No—Yes

Dear Angela,

The questions that follow are defining. You deserve to be treated well. What are your answers?

Does your abuser care about you?

> In the end, I don't think my abuser cared about me except for my usefulness to him. I don't think the abuse was about me. It was about his needs, especially to control.

Do you deserve to be talked to with disrespect, blaming, name-calling, and put-downs?

> I heard a lot of verbal abuse. It was sick. It came from the inside. I tried to understand it.

> What did I deserve? I believed that my behavior merited respect and fair treatment. I tried not to ask for or insist on anything. I excused abuse with nobody's perfect, including me; so try to forgive, move on, and try harder. Sometimes I settled for the crumbs of happiness that

were left. I let myself be used. Being used morphed, and being abused followed as a sneaky intruder.

I was wrong! We need to treat ourselves well. We deserve to be treated well. We need to treat others well.

Do you deserve abuse?

Never!

Do you enjoy being controlled and manipulated?

I didn't. I knew I was capable of making good choices. I knew I was a responsible person. I didn't want to become a weak wimp.

Do you deserve an end to the abuse?
Do you want the abuse to end?
Are you scared?
Does God love you?

Trust God,

Emily

Lost—Where Is Home?

Dear Angela,

Do you wonder where your home is? Abuse creates a homelessness of the heart.

Home is more than shelter. It's more than a place to eat and sleep. It's more than a place to keep your stuff.

Home is where you are loved, can land softly, can be relaxed and enjoy family and friends. Home is where you can share joys and sorrows.

Home is where you're welcome. Home is where you are safe.

For years, where I lived didn't feel like home. Now I live alone. That doesn't mean I'm lonely. I savor the solace. I come and go freely. I have friends and family in often. There are many things I enjoy doing. It is peaceful. I am safe. I have a home.

Keep looking,

Emily

How Are You?

Dear Angela,

Someone asks: "How are you?" You answer: "I am fine." Really?

Of course, we want to be fine. But to say we're fine when we aren't is lying. Don't lie to yourself or others.

I had a list of painful feelings, a list of what I tried to be, and a list of what helped me feel good. Now, I don't think we should share our long lists with everyone. I am sharing them with you because maybe they can help you as you assess who you are. My lists were an internal gauge and guide to manage my feelings and needs. I do think we need to answer truthfully, maybe sharing a need for a listening ear, requesting a prayer, asking how we can help another. I think we need to get over whatever is in the way of "fine."

My painful feelings: ashamed, embarrassed, betrayed, stupid, cheap, belittled, put-down, barely tolerated, disrespected, rejected, frightened, angry, disgusted, lost, discouraged, dismissed, cheated, disappointed, weak, hurt, broken, unappreciated, grieving, sad, defeated, exhausted, unloved, controlled, manipulated, empty, sorry, fragile, wasted, scared, used, abused.

My action plan: to be optimistic and happy, to smile, to laugh, to be faithful, prayerful, helpful, hopeful, kind, loving, flexible and resilient, forgiving, grateful for good, encouraging and supportive, strong and courageous, and to find joy.

My feel-good needs: love, kindness, affirmation, affection, appreciation, honesty, help, rest, hope, faith, prayer, family, friends, encouragement, peace, acceptance, fairness, forgiveness and grace, respect, safety, hope, freedom, smiles, music, laughter, and joy.

How does your pain feel? What is your plan? What makes you feel good? We probably have a lot in common. It is good to recognize our feelings. We need to find balance and healing. Despite our feelings and failures, God loves us, forgives us, and gives us the grace to live life abundantly, even in the midst of abuse.

Be real,

Emily

How Do I Look?

Dear Angela,

Do you ask yourself that question? I think most women do. We want to look good. We want to feel good about ourselves. Abuse changes how we look.

Years ago, I looked in the mirror one day, and what I saw was pain and grief. There was such blankness and emptiness I hardly recognized me. The broken heart changes our posture and countenance. Weariness and sadness get in the way of smiles and joy and laughter. The physical abuse I experienced didn't leave cuts and bruises. Cuts and bruises would have been hard to hide. Tears mess up the makeup. Sometimes we eat too much or too little, and that shows. Our silence is deafening.

Abuse changes how we look at things: there are always options. Do we look to surrender? Do we look to fight for what is right? Do we look for a good flight? Look to God for guidance.

How do I look? Do I have a plan? How can it be better? How will I move on? There is no time for immobility.

After I left, after the divorce, after some healing time, friends told me how different I looked. There were comments about the smiles and joy that were obvious. I was told I always looked so nice, and I was even told I was beautiful. The inner beauty of me was showing. It was a wonderful makeover.

God created us in his own image. How do we look?

Look up,

Emily

Do I Need a Jacket?

Dear Angela,

What do you need for your journey?

Getting ready for the journey was daunting. I wanted to be sure I had what I needed until I got to the freedom destination. I thought about jackets. I'm a basic nonswimmer in the literal sense. As the depths of abuse increased, I knew figuratively that I needed a life jacket. I was in way over my head. My life jacket came with the support of friends, prayer, therapists, and pastors.

When rejection came early and often, I needed an insulated jacket. It was so cold to be pushed out of the marriage. I found that jacket as I found sheltering places for my soul.

I even thought about a flak jacket. Spiritually, emotionally, even physically, I was concerned about safety. I needed real protection to move on bravely and courageously. I needed others to help me and protect me.

I had a half-packed bag for a long time. It was unobtrusive in a closet but ready for a quick exit. It helped me to think about what was essential, what would be helpful, and what was always ready. To want to escape abuse is a biggy, and it's scary.

We have been promised that the Lord will never leave us comfortless. That was the best jacket of all.

Angela, I so hope you can be free from abuse.

Stay safe,

Emily

Thin Ice and Eggshells

Dear Angela,

Are you afraid of the ice? Have you ever stepped on an egg?

My abuser brought fear to me. If I wasn't very careful with what I said or did, it became very cold and dangerous. He tried to make me feel like I was all wet. I had ventured out too far. I should have known better. I was afraid to make choices. He certainly wasn't there to protect or rescue me if I made a bad choice. Any misstep on my part was unfortunate reality for me.

Eggshells were another problem. I learned early on that some eggs have thinner shells than others. Some eggs roll around. Some eggs crack and are messy. Broken eggs leave messy cleanup.

Stay off the ice and the eggshells. There are safer places to walk and certainly better stepping-stones to a healthy, abuse-free journey.

Step carefully,

FLIGHT DELAY

Dear Angela,

One way to end abuse is to arrange for flight.

I can't tell you how many flight delays I had. To even plan a flight was scary. I was ashamed and embarrassed. I wasn't totally sure I wanted to leave. After all, what I wanted wasn't to leave but for the abuse to end.

Many years ago, I finally summoned the courage to call the office of an attorney I knew to ask for a referral to a divorce attorney. I waited until my husband was out of the house to make the call. It was probably too early in the morning, and no one answered the phone. I would try again later ... it didn't happen. Flight delay.

Another time, I was ready to leave when my abuser became seriously ill for months. After hospitalization, during and after rehab, he required 24/7 care. The caregiving and need to lift him along with little sleep caused me great physical pain. My doctors were able to get me some pain relief but informed me that caring for him was too much. Not only was he not grateful for the care, he was abusive and angry with me because I was tired. But I thought it was my responsibility as his wife to stay and care for him. Plans changed. Flight delay.

At another point in the abuse journey, the mental

health issues became so intense that I was ready to leave. I had begged him to get help and for us to get help, but he had refused. He must have figured out that I was on my way out because he finally consented to seek out a therapist. I thought I should give him time to work on this. Flight delay.

He had been very abusive to my family and disliked my friends. Then a time came when he mellowed a little, and I was cautiously optimistic. Maybe there would be better times and more of them. Flight delay.

I thought maybe I could work with a therapist and at least learn better coping skills. Flight delay.

I thought maybe our marriage could be repaired. He refused to work together. But maybe I needed to be patient. Flight delay.

We'd been married for many years. It would cause a lot of pain and be a lot of work to divorce, move, and go our separate ways. Did I have the energy to do this? Flight delay.

The abuse escalated.

I had to find a way to move on without delay. I took flight, and I have arrived safely!

Fly safely,

BE WELL NOURISHED!
FRUIT IS GOOD!

Dear Angela,

   The journey takes energy. Feeding your soul with the biblical fruits of the spirit helps.

   My thoughts:

> Love is like a flower.
>> Hate consumes;
>>> with love, the spirit blooms!

> Joy is like the morning,
>> ever new,
>>> ever bright,
>>>> ever light,
>>>>> to follow night.

> Peace is like a gentle breeze,
>> the absence of storm
>>> but all the energy
>>>> of creation.

> Patience is like a promise,
>> anticipation of fulfillment
>>> and the assurance of faith.

Kindness is like a yield right-of-way sign.
  making way for another's needs and
    taking care of yourself in the process.

Faithfulness is like a flower,
  loyal, constant, trusting, believing,
    and although it withers, falls, and
    goes to seed,
      it rests and rises renewed and
      blossoms again.

Gentleness is like a blossom,
  strong enough to be fragile,
    full of strength to be arrayed in
    beauty.

Self-control is like surrender,
  letting go and
    letting God take over.

Be filled with the spirit,

Emily

DUCKS IN A ROW: COULD
I? SHOULD I? WOULD I?

Dear Angela,

You may want to assess your choices in the face of abuse. Long before I made the decision to leave the abuse, I had been assessing choices and putting my ducks in a row. The beginning was recognizing the abuse wouldn't go away without action. I tried talking with him in a calm, kind, logical, and realistic way. Frustration and anger often interfered. We needed a plan that would work for both of us. If it wouldn't work for one, it wouldn't work for the other.

I shared my frustration with his devaluing me as his wife. I no longer felt loved and appreciated even as just a friend or companion. It broke my heart. I tried to stay committed, to help and be kind. More and more, I felt empty, trapped, and used as a resident housekeeper and caregiver. I was scared. I had become the target of his abusive outbursts and episodes of rage. Being helpful is a gift to another. Using and abusing another is theft.

You already know that I had a half-packed bag. A friend also insisted I have her house key. I did a little attorney shopping online but wasn't confident about a choice. I made sure I understood our finances. It helped to know I could afford to leave. My heart goes out to anyone who is stuck in abuse because it is unaffordable to leave. I prayed. I read. I talked with my doctor. I found a therapist. She was helpful, but she left the practice. I was in acquiescence mode too long after that.

A couple of months before I left, I found another therapist who worked with me to be more assertive and resolve ambivalence. I knew I needed the abuse to end. We addressed my safety. Could I be safe and not leave? One suggestion was to always have my cell phone with me. I slept with it within easy reach.

Clearly, I wanted the abuse to end. Leaving would be one way to end the abuse. Staying was hardly an option. Any sense of romance was gone. My husband knew this. I still felt compassion for him. I believed my marriage vows were a lifelong commitment, and therefore my faith was compelling me to stay. But could I, should I, would I leave my husband? My therapist respected my faith and where I was in my struggle on the journey. He listened. He made suggestions. He encouraged. He helped me plan for the end of abuse. He helped me coordinate a safe exit from abuse, our marriage, and our home.

My close friends were such good listeners and helped me sort through the mess. One Sunday, I arrived at church a little early. My pastor came over and greeted me. I told him I had a prayer request for the abused and their abusers. He gave me a quizzical look. I told him I was in an abusive marriage. He asked me if I was safe. I hesitantly replied, "Probably," but I was so scared. It was dangerous. He asked what help I needed.

A few days later, I was in his office. I desperately needed coping skills. If my conscience wouldn't let me leave, I needed help to stay. As we talked, I said, "I can't take it anymore." He said, "You won't." At first I thought it was semantics. He helped me understand the difference. I had a choice. I think I had been seeking permission to leave. It felt so good to think I did not have to keep taking the abuse.

At my next therapy appointment, I decided that if there was another abusive time, I would leave. We talked about strategy. A few days later, there was another abusive time; that was the day I decided to leave. My therapist helped me negotiate a plan to tell my husband I was leaving.

I called my house-key friend of many years and asked if I could come. She and her husband welcomed me and surrounded me with supportive love, care, and encouragement for several months. The day I arrived at their home, I was emotionally and physically exhausted. There had been little sleep the previous night. I went to bed early and slept the best I had in many years. I was safe.

One part of the long journey was over. I was headed in a new direction. It took strength and courage to leave. The new journey has been so good.

Angela, I do hope you have a plan. With your ducks in a row, you'll know better where to go.

Wishing you safe travel,

Emily

5

Leaving

Frightened. Fear elicits two choices: fight or flight. Fighting seemed futile. Flight seemed like an escape. Leaving meant the end of we and a beginning of just me. For a time, I was afraid to stay and afraid to fly. I still asked God, "Why the ugly abuse?" I asked about the broken promise.

As divorce became reality, I began to understand covenant promise. Marriage promises are a twosome. Eventually I understood what it was to be forgiven and free.

911
Point of No Return
Whereabouts Unknown
Keeping a Promise
Two to Make, One to Break
Time to Go—Port of Last Resort

911

Dear Angela,

Are you thinking that abuse and anger are just part-time? When you live in a storm path, devastation often follows. Storms come through sometimes predictably and sometimes not. Full-time awareness of danger is required. For me, the abusive anger and rage became intolerable. Rage! I didn't know about excessive, abusive anger. Rage was a totally new experience.

Many times, I was very frightened. In one journal entry, I wondered if I should leave that night. But where would I go? Sometimes I wrote about taking a time-out and going out to get away and be safe until the storm and rage passed. I wanted to run away. I had friends and family who would help me. I worked on a safety plan for me, which ultimately was to leave.

I could often sense the volcano of anger rising. Most often, the anger and rage happened at home. There were outbursts in public places too. It happened at the mall, at church, before a concert, at a restaurant, even in his doctor's office. Trying to be logical with the angry abuser is illogical. Even when my husband was told certain behaviors would mean a 911 call, and land him in jail or hospitalized, he was unconvinced. You can't reason with rage.

Professionals involved encouraged me to call 911. They thought it was a safety plan for me, and it could have been. It often seemed like the best option until I thought about the aftermath. If I called 911, he might settle down before help arrived. If they came and they got him settled down and left, I would be left with an angry man ready to rage again. If they came and took him elsewhere, it probably wouldn't be long before he regained composure, and he would be sent home. In each of the scenarios, I would have yet another problem to face, backlash in the aftermath.

When you are scared to be home or anywhere because of the abusive anger and rage of another, it's time to not be with that person. I believed that if my husband couldn't help the way he treated me, that was so sad; and if he could and didn't want to treat me well, that hurt even more. No one can be responsible for an abuser's behavior. Abusers lack empathy and compassion. The abuser does not care about you and your well-being. The abuser needs to own responsibility for the abusive behavior.

Be careful and be safe,

POINT OF NO RETURN

Dear Angela,

Have you ever thought about leaving and not going back? Even when I fled to the safety of my friends' home, I still wondered if separation was an option. I did know I could no longer live at the same address. How could I share this decision with him? An e-mail wouldn't be good, and a telephone call seemed cowardly. I needed to tell him in person. I felt so insecure and scared. My therapist had cautioned me not to go alone. His caution was merited.

There was no suitable family or friend option. I wished I had a brother to accompany me, but I don't have a brother. I decided to ask my pastor if he would consider going with me. He agreed; he told me everyone needs an advocate. A time was set, and the three of us met. It was difficult to tell my husband that it wouldn't work for us to live at the same address any longer. I told him that although the romance was gone, I still felt compassion and commitment to him. I assured him I had some fond memories for which I was very grateful. My pastor was very professional and kind. Before we left, we shared resource connections with my husband.

In the next few days, I struggled with the choice and

my exhaustion. I was emotionally spent but spiritually much stronger. A friend went with me to get clothes and documents a few days later. It was one of the most stressful, frightening experiences of my life. My husband vacillated between wanting to talk, with me alone, to telling me his therapist said I had no right to be there. He began talking about the police to get me out of there. As quickly as possible, I got the most important documents, medications, and a limited wardrobe together. What I left with that day was what I had until much later when another friend went with me to help pack for the move to my new place. That trip back to the safety of my friends' home made the separation or divorce choice more obvious.

The heartache was nearly overwhelming. He called frequently with lots of requests for me to reconsider, with more abuse even in the same conversation. I soon shut my cell off at night. I knew that asking me to return was not because he loved me and was sorry. Most likely it was because I would be useful, convenient, and inexpensive help. At one point, he asked if there was someone else in my life. "No." Would I ever remarry? "No." Every bit of abusive talk and behavior only made me more confident about choosing divorce.

Choose wisely,

WHEREABOUTS UNKNOWN

Dear Angela,

Would you feel safer with your whereabouts unknown? I certainly did.

When I went to my friends' home for refuge, I only planned to be there very briefly until I could find a short-term lease or go to an extended-stay hotel. It also seemed possible that I would return home. My husband had been so dependent upon my help that it seemed likely he could not live alone. Long story short, he began managing quite well.

Before I left, I e-mailed family, friends, and others who needed to contact me. My cell was the only way to contact me. Eventually I had e-mail access again. A forwarding address for mail was not an option. I wanted to be whereabouts unknown.

For the next several months, I was in semi-seclusion. Few knew where I was. I never told my husband where I was. I was still teaching part-time and continued to drive to teach in the former neighborhood. I continued to worship at my church and volunteer there. I drove a lot of miles. I had the safety of distance and the freedom to function in my usual life.

Soon after I left, I contacted an attorney recommended

by a friend. We talked about separation or divorce. I chose divorce.

Living with my friends felt like God was hugging me, protecting me, and showing me how to live in freedom and safety. Their background was social work and ministry. Was I in good hands? Wow! We spent many hours talking and listening. They were supportive of my decision. She helped me maintain equilibrium and not get too caught up trying to reason with my husband. They helped me get through sadness and guilt.

God always knows our whereabouts.

Accept help,

Emily

KEEPING A PROMISE

Dear Angela,

You are likely struggling with the pain of broken promise. Trust me; the pain is real, but it does get better. As I left the abusive marriage, I struggled with my beliefs about compassion and commitment. It felt wrong to abandon compassion and commitment. My new understanding is more through the eyes of grace than the eyes of law. Through grace, I have experienced God loving me and freeing me to live in joy and blessing.

This is how I now understand compassion. Compassion and empathy are intertwined in loving another. To be compassionate demands honesty. It is real, personal, loving, warm, and caring. Compassion can also be felt for strangers and even those we don't like. It may be less personal but still very real, full of human kindness and caring. In the later years, my compassion for my husband was still very real, but it had become quite an impersonal ritual of kindness, caring, and concern. I felt guilty for not caring for him out of a warm and loving spirit but simply out of duty. I asked God to forgive me.

Our marriage vows were typical. We promised to love and be faithful through the good and bad as long as we lived. When I make a promise, I try to keep my word. Over and over, I asked God to show me the way to keep the promise.

I wasn't the only one who made a promise that day so long ago. It was a covenant commitment. It was a together promise. When the covenant promise was no longer a twosome commitment, the marriage could not survive.

I am learning to commit my way unto the Lord and trust in him. God always keeps his promises to his children, and he will show us the way!

Trust in the Lord,

Emily

Two to Make, One to Break

Dear Angela,

Breaking the abuse cycle and moving on is a tough job. Healing takes lots of work. It's a little like cleaning up the mess and repairing storm damage. In assessing the deterioration of our marriage, the escalation of abuse, the need to move in a new direction, I searched for reasons and understanding. I tried not to make excuses for either of us. I've forgiven him and wish him well. That doesn't mean I condone the abuse. It was evil. Forgiving doesn't mean forgetting what happened.

An egalitarian marriage is a covenant commitment. Our two-way commitment had been destroyed. I never suspected adultery or the unfaithfulness of an affair. There had been other betrayal, and pornography was part of the betrayal. Hardness of heart had led to abuse. I so wanted the commitment fixed. A two-way effort to fix didn't happen.

In searching the scriptures about divorce, I read literally, missing the foundation of underlying grace. I allowed myself a distorted and exaggerated sense of my ability and responsibility to make the marriage work and see to it there was no divorce. I wanted to fix it by myself. How arrogant! Unrealistic! Not possible!

Now I think about it this way:

> Two to make, one to break.
> Two to fix, one to nix.
> Two-way or no way.

Pray for healing,

Emily

Time to Go—Port
of Last Resort

Dear Angela,

Do you just want the abuse to end?

That was at the top of my want list / wish list. Eventually it was at the top of my needs list: no more weeds, no more confusion of wants and needs. Sometimes I just wanted to run away. I even told him so, and it didn't seem to matter to him. He was in control.

Abusive behavior is never right. It is selfish and evil. It is destructive to both the abuser and abused. No one deserves to be abused. No one has the right to abuse. One person can't always be right or always be the only winner. Unless both are winners together, no one wins. With abuse, no one wins.

The abuser is the only one who can stop the abusive behavior. The recipient/victim can be prayerful, patient, flexible, and supportive. But if the abuser won't stop or can't stop, it's time for the abused to take back control. It's time to go.

It took me so long to wrap my head and my heart around the decision to divorce. Even when I was so soundly rejected, betrayed, belittled, disregarded, dismissed, used, and abused, I kept thinking that we were still married. Now, I think we weren't married for many years. Spiritual and emotional divorce operate on a different platform and a different timetable than the public and legal process. I think it was wrong for me not to leave when it clearly was over. It was a façade, and a façade is a lie.

Divorce is ugly. I am sorry that abuse led to divorce. The abuse has ended. I am no longer a resident target. Leaving was the right choice, and I would do it again in a heartbeat. It was a profound loss. There was profound sadness. I wept when the divorce was final. There are times when I still feel a little sad, a little empty, and a little apprehensive. But I am free, and I am safe. I can smile, laugh, and be joyful.

I am thankful and blessed. Wow!

Blessings on your journey!

Emily

6

Transition

Separation. When together ends and separate begins, it is not without some overlap. It is not a matter-of-fact time. Transition demands letting go. It is time to set aside the pain. It is also a time to remember the good. It is time to anticipate freedom and responsibility in a new way. It too is part of the journey to the blessing of healing.

You Found Me—I Wasn't Looking for You
Detach Here
Try to Remember
What Did They Say?

You Found Me—I Wasn't Looking for You

Dear Angela,

Are you afraid of your abuser? Or maybe just not wanting to be in the same place at the same time?

In a good relationship, absence can make the heart grow fonder. In the aftermath of abuse, absence makes my heart feel safer. As I told you in an earlier letter, I was mostly whereabouts unknown to my husband. He wasn't told where I lived, but he did know some of my activity.

One Sunday shortly after I left, my husband, who hadn't been to church in a very long time, appeared directly in front of me, facing me where I was seated. It seemed like he was in both my face and space. He greeted me and tried to be pleasant as he delivered his handwritten messages to me. When he left, the friend I was sitting with asked, "Who was that?" She had met him long before but didn't recognize him. It was quite an incredulous experience. Later, when I went to get my coat in another area, he was standing at an opposite doorway, clearly looking for me. I tried to move so he wouldn't find me. He left. I left later. I felt stalked.

Weeks later, I was at a mall shopping on a level where he would not normally be. I turned, and there he was. He said he had seen me, recognized my gait, and followed me. He asked about my shopping. I left as quickly as possible.

There were other times when the coincidence of meeting him, like in a mall parking lot, seemed strange. One day at a grocery store, I was getting items from a freezer. Again, I turned, and there he was in the middle of the aisle, in my face and space. He announced, "You found me." I replied, "I wasn't looking for you."

I try to avoid "coincidence."

Stay safe,

Emily

DETACH HERE

Dear Angela,

"Detach here."

When I get this message, I know that someone, some organization, some cause wants me to take action. It might be a payment request, a donation request, or perhaps an invitation to an opportunity that needs an RSVP. It is a choice and responsibility to detach.

After a property settlement had been reached and the court granted the divorce, it was as though I missed "detach here." As I moved into the healing process, my therapist suggested that I was not emotionally divorced. I needed to detach.

The divorce settlement had been difficult. Near the end of the process it had become a bully battle that I could not afford to fight. There were several matters that needed to be addressed and resolved fairly. My husband made negotiating a challenge. He said he didn't care if the additional cost was enormous and if it took another year or two to reach a settlement. I decided to cut my losses and move on courageously. Before the divorce was final, we had verbally agreed on a division of the estimated income taxes which had been paid from joint accounts prior to the divorce. He would later renege on this agreement.

There was lingering abuse after the divorce as we tried to reach an agreement on the estimated tax issue. Telephone calls followed which were often very negative and abusive monologues. These calls were not helpful. He was in filibuster mode and threatened to be nasty. He would later change the subject to share his self-pity party pain and make requests. He would ask me to reconsider and give him one more chance. He suggested lunch. He wanted to see my place. I denied these requests. The calls were disturbing. To end each long harassing call I would tell him I was hanging up, and I did.

I stopped answering his many calls. He did not leave messages. The calls were an extension of the control issues in our relationship. It was frightening. I filed a police report. The detective who worked the case said the cycle of control had to be broken. The boundary had to be firmly established. There was concern that the abusive behavior would escalate. A case was opened and law enforcement intervention was effective. It gave me a renewed sense of safety and freedom.

Once the abuse was over. I needed to detach. He was no longer my responsibility. It didn't mean I'd lost empathy or compassion for him as another person God created. It did mean that I must let go and let God.

Angela, it's hard to separate, to detach completely.

If this is what you need to do, it is good to have help. I was amazed at all of the resources available and the many people who helped me. My prayer support team included folks I'd known well for years. It also included folks I didn't know well but who learned of the struggle and reached out to me in love. It's hard for me to ask for help. But I did ask for help as I navigated the transition. The response was overwhelming, like they thought it was a privilege for them to be helping me.

I've forgiven my former husband for the abuse. I wish him no ill. In fact, I want only the best for him. I want him to be able to accept God's love and grace and forgiveness. I want him to have hope and peace.

To completely detach was an enormously important choice and responsibility. It was difficult. Healing is easier now with an end to the many years of abuse. It is truly a time for thanksgiving.

Angela, ask for help if you need it. Trust God to help you know who to ask for help. It is a privilege to help others. When we ask for help, we give another the privilege of giving help where help is needed.

Let others help you,

Try to Remember

Dear Angela,

Even in the midst of abuse, there can be a window of wonderful, a respite from the pain. When I found our life especially painful, I would try to remember the good. It helped me realize that there had been good times. I hadn't married and never known good.

My prayer was for the strength to be kind and forgiving. I asked for help to remember that no matter how ugly I felt about the relationship, the Lord created and loves me, and the Lord also created and loves my former husband.

Now in the healing process, I also recall some of the fond memories. I am very grateful. We traveled in the United States and Canada. We went to the Caribbean and Mexico. We made fall leaf tour drives. There were concerts, movies, dinner theater, and Sunday brunch after church. We enjoyed gardening and the farmer's market. One year he made a from-scratch German chocolate cake for my birthday. He rented movies for me when I had a nasty tummy bug.

We had several favorite restaurants. Yummy times. I especially recall one quaint and elegant restaurant far from home. It wasn't expensive, but it was as though we had been transported to another world of tranquility and beauty.

He would tell me he was proud of me. He was affectionate. Tender touch was beautiful. He spoke kindly. What a blessing words of encouragement were. One time we were shopping. In her friendly southern way, the clerk addressed me as "sweetheart." He was standing nearby, heard her, and in a most genuine and endearing way said, "She's *my* sweetheart."

The fond memories of the years together are a continued blessing.

I don't understand why there are only memories.

Treasure the good times.

Blessings to you,

Emily

What Did They Say?

Dear Angela,

What will they say? Does it matter?

Are you wondering what folks will say if and when you leave the abuse? I certainly wondered if others would respond with loud silence or perhaps a carefully worded negative statement. I thought there would be some who would say they hoped it would get better ... I expected some rejection. I didn't expect exuberant affirmation.

What they said was surprising and hardly believable.

They told me I was strong and courageous. And I had felt so weak and wimpy.

They told me I was right to leave. Enough was enough.

They told me they were proud of me. This sounded so good to me. I work with children and had been so concerned about the bad example I was setting in divorcing. This helped me realize that I was setting a good example by refusing to accept abuse in my life.

They told me I had made the right choice! I thought of divorce as failure. How could they see that failure as the right choice? They helped me understand that staying so long was wrong.

What did they say? It mattered.

I have been blessed.
God is good!

Listen carefully,

Emily

7

Blessed

Imagine this! Decades of abuse ended. It was hard to be patient when the struggle seemed unending. God's time is best!

The healing process continues with each new day. These final letters are about joy and the abundant blessings that followed.

Am I Broken?
Home at Last
Bedrock and Beautiful
Grieving and Airlifted
Older and Newer
Blessed—God's Forever Love
Joy—Laughter—Hugs—Healing

AM I BROKEN?

Dear Angela,

Maybe you have asked yourself that question too. I knew I was, and I so wanted to be rescued. Are we ever broken beyond repair? No way! There's use for the broken, the brokenhearted. It's a wonderful gift. I was taught this verse as a child. I often reflect on it for soul repair.

For by grace you have been saved through faith, and this is not your own doing; it is the gift of God—not the result of works, so that no one may boast. (Ephesians 2:8–9 NRSV)

Take Another Look!

Sometimes I look at life and all its goals and dreams.
    Some never happened;
        some turned catastrophic and painful.
Shattered dreams are like shattered glass.

I'll take another look in the light.

Shattered glass reflects so differently
and often so more beautifully,
like a prism designed and cut for
another use.

A light catcher,

beautiful, intriguing, ever changing!

Look again,

Emily

HOME AT LAST

Dear Angela,

We all deserve to have a real home. Do you ever feel like you are homeless at home? When I moved into my own place after the abuse, I knew I had a home for the first time in a very long time. It was the perfect place!

During many years of marriage, there had been far too many times when I was not permitted to have my family come to visit. When they were there, it had to be brief, and once he told me to have them leave a few hours after they arrived. He promised ugliness if they didn't. One Christmas some of my family and I had a meal together at a mall restaurant. Then we went to the mall parking lot and opened gifts in the car.

Another time, my family planned to come to celebrate my birthday. I had asked if this was okay, and he had agreed. He changed his mind and insisted that I un-invite them. He mostly ignored me that day. I cried most of that day. The hurt was profound.

My friends were not really welcome at the house either. It was always plan carefully, keep it low-key, and more often meet friends elsewhere.

The house was never home.

Steps were a problem for both of us. We moved to a one-level condo a few months before I left him. It was very nice and easier living. When I left, I thought I would be returning to the condo and he would be living elsewhere. He hadn't liked the condo and complained bitterly. But as we sorted out our lives before the divorce, he decided he didn't want to move.

Despite how nice it was, there were things I didn't like. When he chose to stay, I rejoiced that I didn't have to deal with the many windows that I couldn't get to appear sparkling clean. The underground parking was no fun either. I would move! The search began.

My realtor asked what I needed. It had to be one level and located near where I teach part-time. Finally, we found a place in not quite the location I wanted and not quite what I wanted. However, it seemed workable, one level, street-level garage, and affordable. My offer, which was negotiated to over list price, was accepted pending housing inspection. Long story short, the furnace, windows, and some appliances were problematic. Lots of expense to fix, and the seller's counter was unacceptable. My realtor thought it was not a good counter. I canceled the purchase agreement.

Just that morning, I had looked online for property in the area where I wanted to live. I told my agent, and very shortly we were viewing my current home. Instantly it felt like home. An offer was made just below list and accepted. One level, street-level garage, immaculate, no housing inspection issues, no carpet (I hate vacuuming). It was so much more home than the others I'd seen. The cost was far below what I thought was realistic. What a blessing. It was as though what I didn't get in our property settlement had been given to me in this housing find.

I had lived with friends for months and wanted to move yesterday. This property was mine in just over three weeks. The owner was caring and generous. She left information about the building, lots of welcoming gestures, including cleaning supplies, toilet paper, lightbulbs, plants, even a bathroom towel. It was clean. I didn't need to even wipe off a cupboard shelf. Kindness is a blessing.

I had struggled with abuse so long. We always had nice places to live. That's not the same as having a home. I wanted a home. I have a home, a perfect place.

On the day the movers came, I was not alone. The friends who had helped with the final packing and retrieval of computer documents also came to be with me on moving day. I had been advised not to be alone. I was so grateful for their help and presence. Peace, quiet, clarity, and focus all came with the move and settling in safely. Shortly after the move, the divorce was final. I am savoring the solace, the freedom from abuse, and the many joys of home.

Angela, I hope that you can know the freedom from abuse, the blessings of home where you are safe and happy. Everyone deserves that perfect place called home.

Anticipate freedom and home,

Emily

BEDROCK AND BEAUTIFUL

Dear Angela,

Do you ever feel like you're walking in the mud, on the ice, on hot sand? Are you walking a steep incline, or maybe it feels like you slipped into a deep ravine? Does it seem unbearably hot? Hypothermia is dangerous too. We do have choices. A couple of months before I left, I had decided that the abuse had to end. He could stop the abuse. Or if I left, I would not be an available target.

I chose to pursue freedom. There would be no more imprisonment of my heart and soul, no more living in fear of escalating abusive anger and rage, and no more being a victim. I wrote this in my journal.

Freedom!

Now I want to embark on the freedom journey.

I want to be free to think, to feel, to be the best person I can be.

I want to be free from guilt, from cowardice, from arrogance.

I want to be free to laugh, to love, to learn.

I want to be free from abuse.

To do this, I needed to find the bedrock of my life. Simply put: God's Son has made me free. To be free is amazing, and when you are on bedrock, you have the firm foundation you need to build a healthy faith and life.

Months after the divorce was final and as the healing began, I heard many comments about how I looked. There were comments about how nice I looked. Interesting, my clothing choices and grooming habits hadn't changed. More than once, I was told I was beautiful. Interesting, my weight hadn't changed. A few more wrinkles are visible. It was certainly surprising.

Remember when I told you that when the abuse escalated seriously, I had looked in the mirror and hardly recognized me because I saw pain, grief, blankness, and emptiness? Our heart shows in our posture and countenance. That is probably why others commented about my appearance and even mentioned beauty. I do feel inner beauty and joy. I smile, I laugh, I enjoy life, and I am blessed. Apparently, it shows.

Bedrock is a firm foundation, and freedom is beautiful.

Wishing you well,

GRIEVING AND AIRLIFTED

Dear Angela,

Abuse is too heavy to carry alone. Grieving is hard work. Long before we divorced, I felt the heavy load of grief. There was sadness that our life together that started out well was becoming painful and joyless. The loss of our hopes and dreams was enormous. Living, loving, caring, and sharing were being replaced by ugliness. There were many good things and fine times that got crowded out of our marriage by a pervasive negative attitude that fueled anxiety and depression. This morphed into abusive anger and rage.

Part of the grief was from feeling like a failure. I was ashamed and embarrassed. I felt so fragile. I tried to bring my prayers of grief to the Lord. God's time is best. Sometimes I wondered when that would be. I felt grief because my husband found life so difficult. Divorce wasn't in either of our game plans. I'm not sure that abuse was his plan either. It was an evil reality. I grieved over the abuse.

How long the grieving will last, I don't know. Now it is about the loss of what might have been. When we married, I expected to love and be loved, to work through differences in a respectful, helpful way. I expected to encourage and be encouraged, to comfort and be comforted, to be honest and caring, and to be affectionate and kind. I planned to love him as long as I lived. I expected us to grow old together.

It will get better. There will be less grieving. Christ promised the yolk would be easy and the burden light. If you try it alone, it's too heavy. The yolk is easy for only one reason: Christ carries the burden. It's time to trust, to be still and know. It's never too late to grow up. Get help! Expect God to show up! You won't be disappointed.

What is a blessing? Always it is God's gift. A blessing is always good. In my healing the hurt journey, I am so humbled and awed by blessings. Blessings sustain, protect, and guide. Blessings are healing and energizing.

A blessing is a glorious airlift!

Anticipate blessing,

Emily

OLDER AND NEWER

Dear Angela,

Abuse ages. But we can learn from it. We can be making a new journey.

For the new to grow, the old must go. Paul says the old in us is evidenced in the hatefulness of insults, lies, anger, and the like. The new in us is seen in the power of gentleness, in compassion, kindness, humility, patience, tolerance, and in forgiveness. In Christ, we are a new creation.

New is never having been before, fresh, unusual, beginning again. What is new? Is the water we drink new? What about the water in the shower? In the waterfall? In the gutter? Water is always in process, always becoming. Water is the great recycling process of all time and place.

The water Moses got when he struck the rock, the water Noah used to float a boat, the water Christ turned into wine at a wedding, the water of Jesus's baptism, of our baptism, is the same water. Water becomes new in the process; it doesn't become older. It is renewed, as are we.

In *The Way* translation of Revelation 21:15, the text is "See, I am making all things new," a new heaven, a new earth, a new Jerusalem, and a new you. It's not "I made" or even "I make" but "I am making"; it's always the process of becoming new. We're not getting older; we're getting newer if we allow ourselves to be new persons in Christ. How exciting!

Think about it. Something is new, newer, newest. It's like this. As we age, we have more and more new experiences. If I'm older than another person, I have had more new experiences, so that makes me newer. Perhaps that means that the oldest person could be the newest?

Angela, there is life after abuse. Abuse must go. Allow yourself to be free to be renewed, newer than you have ever been before.

Be refreshed. Be renewed,

Emily

BLESSED—GOD'S FOREVER LOVE

Dear Angela,

Maybe you wonder who you are. When the abuse hangs especially heavy, it's easy to ask, "What's wrong with me?" I asked myself that question so many times. I didn't feel worthy. I didn't want to be worthless. I wanted to remain humble but certainly not humiliated. I also knew I was not some awful person who deserved to be used and abused. I'm okay. I'm a good person created in God's image. It's good to stand tall.

It's good to bow down and ask for forgiveness. When we pray for forgiveness, our guilt is lifted. We know that all things work together for good with those who love God. It's not easy to love your enemy and pray for the one who hurts you. Were those years of abuse and pain wasted and lost? No, God's plan is best, and God's time is best. When you are free and forgiven, you will find the strength and gentleness to live life wholly.

Forgiving as we are forgiven is a requirement. Vengeance belongs to the Lord. There can be no eye for an eye. The Lord repays with love's revenge. We are called to love as we are loved. That's more than getting even. That's winning. That's redeemed. It's forever!

You are free,

Emily

JOY—LAUGHTER—
HUGS—HEALING

Dear Angela,

I don't know where you are in your life journey. There will be changes. Some things are game changers. If you're struggling, it helps to find joy in something or with someone. Joy is like the sunrise shedding light on the new day and new way.

Laughter—what a wonderful juxtaposition of wit and wisdom, a true celebration of life's resiliency. Look and listen and then experience the joy of laughter. Laugh exuberantly! Doesn't it feel good?

Hugs! Source of renewable energy and hope. We all need hugs. Giving or receiving a hug is a gift. When you are hugged, you are not alone. Sharing a hug is healing. Go for it!

It would be easy to say that our long marriage should never have been, but it was, it hurt, and it ended. I don't understand abuse. I don't understand why. I do know that God has not stopped loving either of us and never will. God loves the sinner but hates the sin. Healing! It feels so good!

The grieving is subsiding. There are fewer tears.

I'm savoring the solace, peace, and freedom of my home. It is such a joy to have my daughter and son and their families here often. I am so proud of them. The grandchildren are so very special. I treasure my family and friends. I'm doing new things, meeting new people. My faith community is awesome. It's good to be free to be me. My faith will sustain me with help and healing. In whatever time I have left, I will move on quietly and gently. It's great to be joyful, forgiven, free, thankful, and blessed.

Ultimately, I believe God hugs us, holds us tight, and heals our hurt. Thanks be to God!

You deserve a hug,

Emily

EPILOGUE

Why these letters? Were the many years living with abuse wasted? What could I do to give back, to pay forward, to help, to heal? I have been so abundantly blessed. In the months following the divorce, I began writing a book, including excerpts from years of journaling and journeying. I knew there were useful things to share. As I wrote, the book became too cumbersome and just plain heavy reading. I stopped.

Shortly afterward, a childhood friend asked if I was still writing. I told her I had decided that it wasn't the way to go. I thought about our conversation. Should I reconsider writing?

It continues to amaze me how God calls us to action. A few nights later, I awakened from a dream in the middle of the night. In the dream, I was mentally writing these letters. It was a format I had never even considered. It was a compelling idea. I was eager to get up and write!

Printed in the United States
By Bookmasters